EDWIN McLE

Miniatures

BOOK 2

Notes from the Publisher

Composers In Focus is a series of original piano collections celebrating the creative artistry of contemporary composers. It is through the work of these composers that the piano teaching repertoire is enlarged and enhanced.

It is my hope that students, teachers, and all others who experience this music will be enriched and inspired.

Frank J. Hackinson, Publisher

Notes from the Composer

Miniatures, Book 2 is an artistic collection of late-elementary/early-intermediate piano solos for students of all ages. In this collection, easy key signatures are introduced, as well as eighth notes and legato pedaling; octaves and difficult leaps have been avoided.

Miniatures, Book 2 features a wide variety of images and moods. Some of the compositions are modern (without being dissonant), while others reflect a historical style. All of the pieces are designed to be a pathway to the standard classical literature.

Edwin McLean

FF1407

Contents

Valse Triste

Edwin McLean

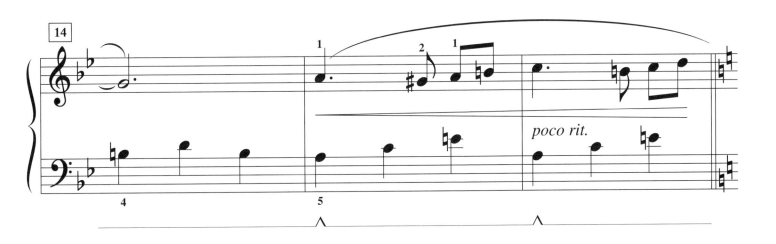

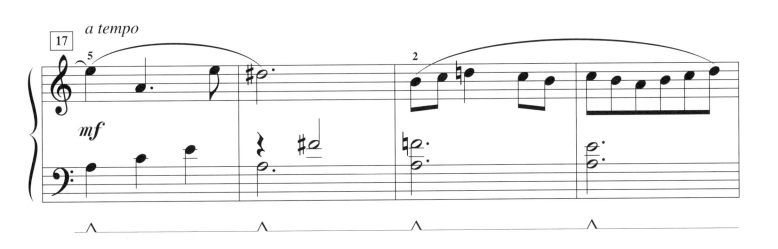

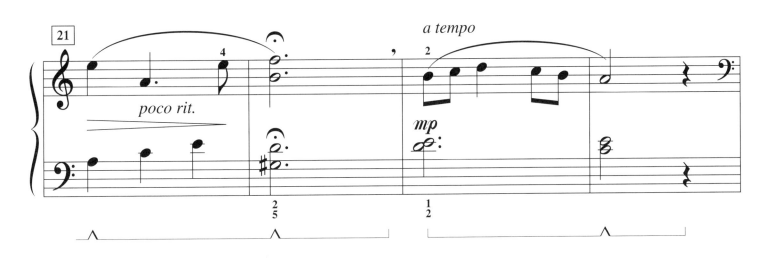

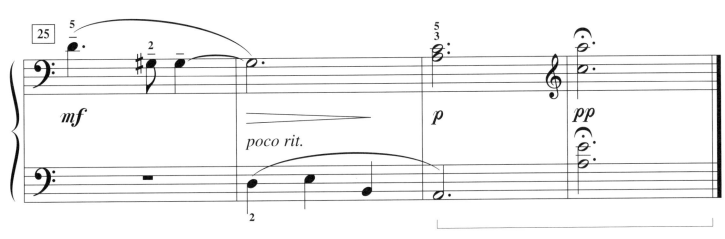

Scherzo Furioso

Forceful and rhythmic (♩ = ca. 108)

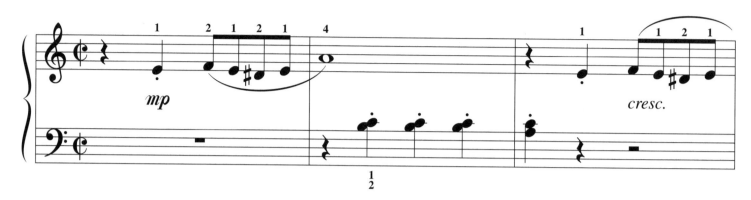

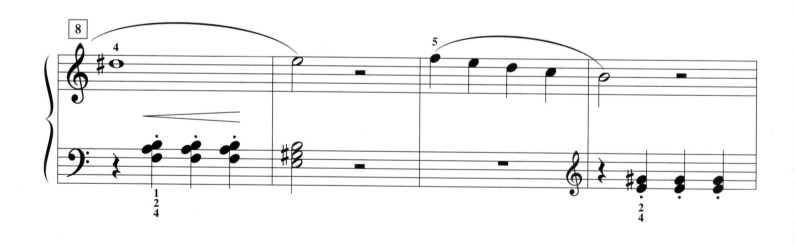

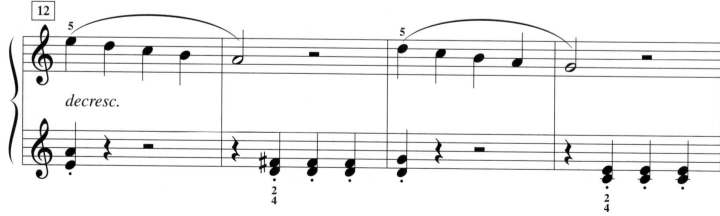

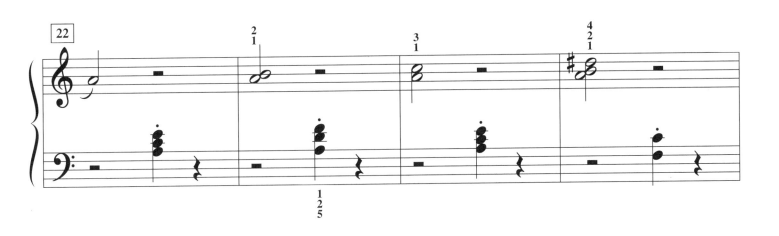

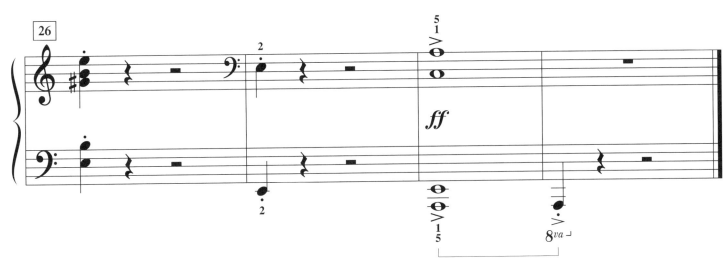

Peaceful Valley

Snowfall Over Mt. Fuji

From a distance

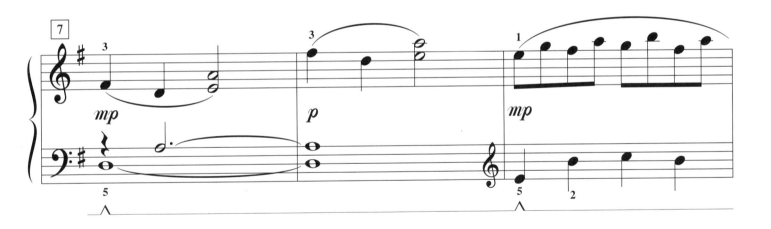

The Gladiator

Powerfully ($\d$ = ca. 92)

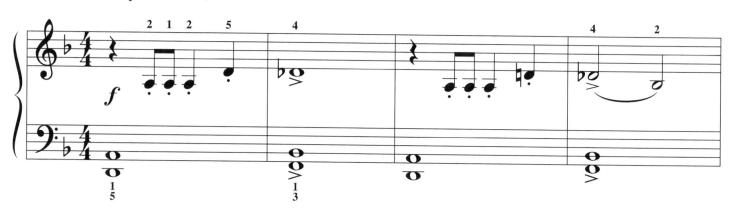

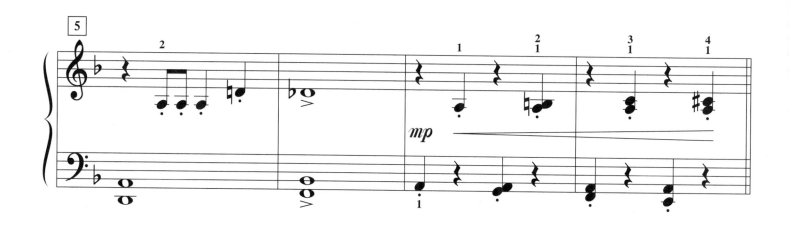

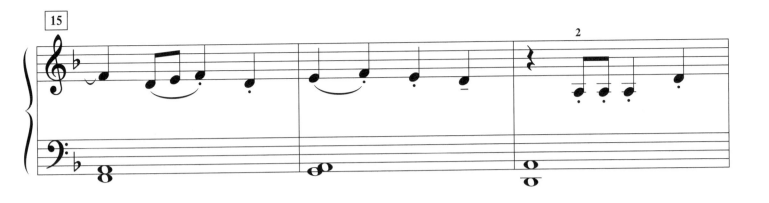

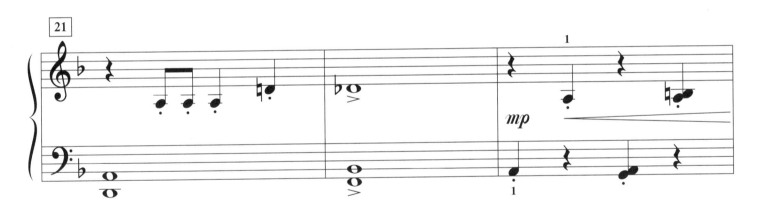

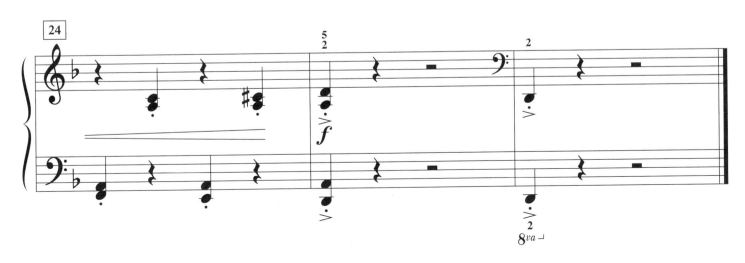

Air in the Baroque Style

Harvest Dance

Allegro (♩ = ca. 116)

Spanish Guitar

Very rhythmic ($\quarternote$ = ca. 168)

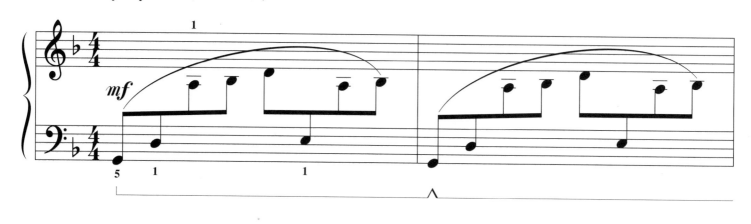

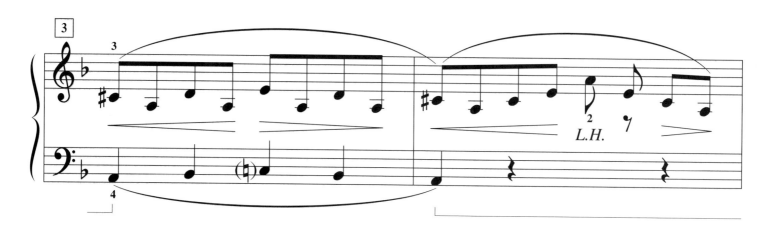

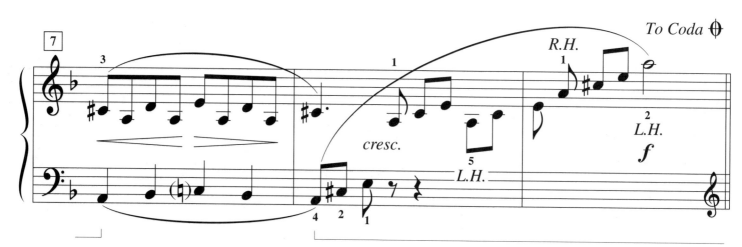

Hymn

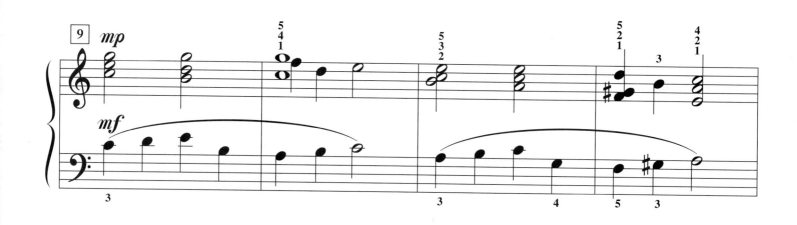

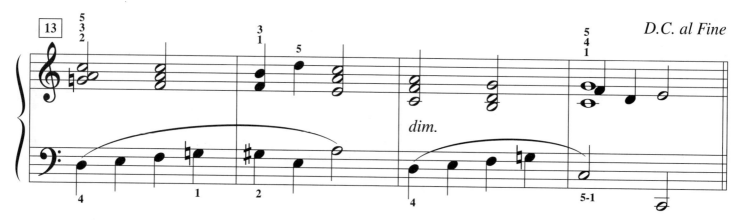

Ballad

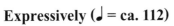

Expressively (♩ = ca. 112)

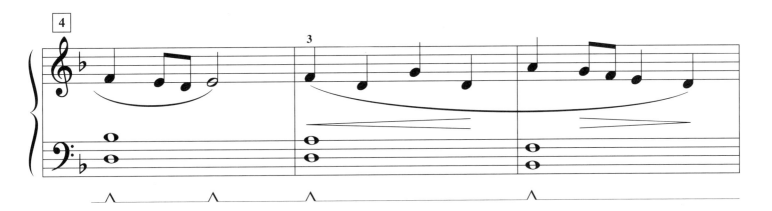

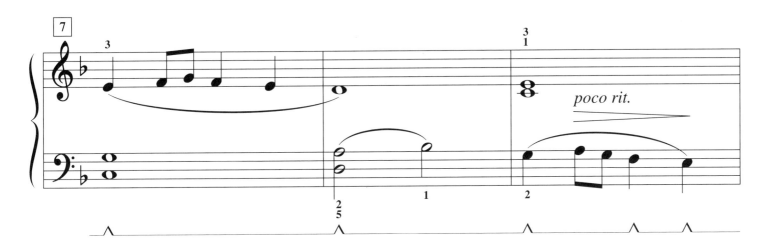

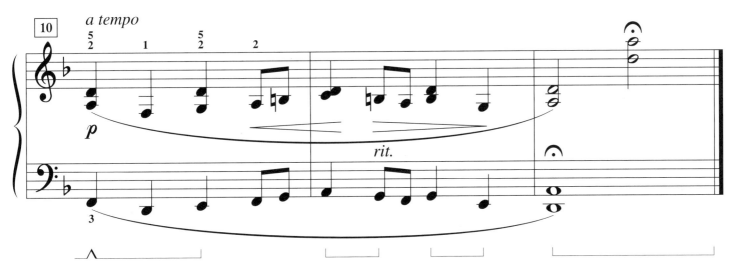

18

The Cello Speaks

Moderato con moto (♩ = ca. 152)

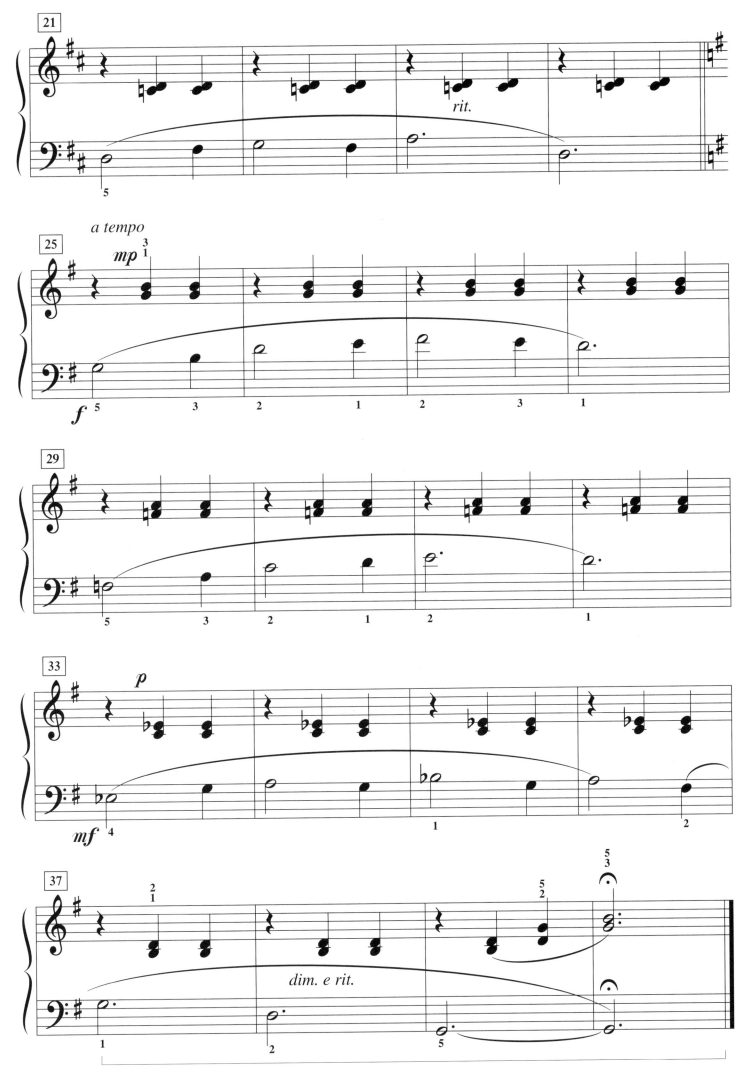

Presto in 5/8

Animato (♩ = ca. 160 or faster)

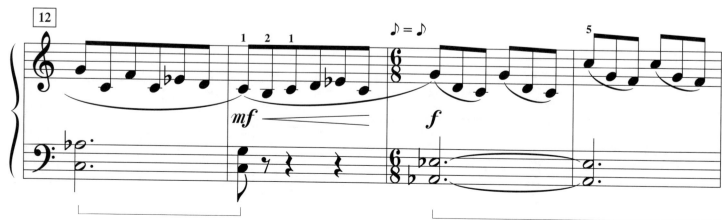

22

Repose